THE HAIRS OF YOUR HEAD NUMBERED

Metropolitan Tabernacle Pulpit.

THE HAIRS OF YOUR HEAD NUMBERED

A Sermon

PREACHED BY

CHARLES H. SPURGEON

AT THE METROPOLITAN TABERNACLE, NEWINGTON.

UPDATED TO MODERN LANGUAGE BY CHARLES J. DOE

CURIOSMITH

MINNEAPOLIS

Published by Curiosmith.
Minneapolis, Minnesota.
Internet: curiosmith.com.

Previously published by PASSMORE & ALABASTER.

The text of this edition is from sermon number 2005, Volume 34 of *The Metropolitan Tabernacle Pulpit,* 1888.

The text was updated to modern equivalents of Elizabethan and Victorian words and phrases. Occasional occurrences of lengthy sentences and close punctuation were left unchanged.

The "Guide to the Contents" was added to this edition by the publisher.

ISBN 9781941281079

GUIDE TO THE CONTENTS

——◦◦⦂◎⦂◦◦——

THE HAIRS OF YOUR HEAD NUMBERED

A SERMON BY

CHARLES H. SPURGEON

But the very hairs of your head are all numbered.
—MATTHEW 10:30.

I t is most delightful to see how familiarly our Lord Jesus talked with his disciples. He was very great, and yet he was among them as one that serves. He was very wise, but he was gentle as a nurse with her children. He was very holy, and far above their sinful infirmities, but he condescended to people of low estate. He was their Master and Lord, and yet their friend and servant. He talked with them, not as a superior who domineers, but as a brother full of tenderness and sympathy. You know how sweetly he once said to them, "If it were not so, I would have told you,"[1] and so he proved that he had hidden nothing from them that was profitable to them. He laid bare his very heart

1 See John 14:2.

to them—his secret was with them. He loved them to the highest degree, and caused the full river of his life to flow for their advantage.

Now, in this chapter, if you read it at home, you will see how wisely the Lord Jesus deals with their fears. He is afraid that they might be afraid; anxious that they would not be anxious, so he talks to them as a very tender friend would talk to some very nervous person—some weak-minded brother or sister—and he speaks in such a way that if they were not comforted, surely they must have willfully resolved not to be comforted. He says to them, "Do not be afraid of those who kill the body but cannot kill the soul. Rather, be afraid of the One who can destroy both soul and body in hell. Are not two sparrows sold for a penny? Yet not one of them will fall to the ground apart from the will of your Father. And even the very hairs of your head are all numbered. So don't be afraid; you are worth more than many sparrows."[1] Brothers and sisters, admire the tenderness of our Lord Jesus and imitate it. Let us try to be equally kind to our fellow Christians. Let us never attempt to show off, or to make ourselves somebody, or to exhibit our strength of faith, for that will grieve the tender little ones, and make them shrink into self-criticism. Let us consider their weakness, and the help that we can provide for them; their sorrow, and the comfort that we can

1 Matthew 10:28–31 (NIV).

afford them. Jesus was himself a Comforter, or he could not have spoken of "another Comforter," and so let us be comforters to our own extent, walking in his steps.

This reminds me, also, to say how very plain and simple the Savior's talk became with his disciples in consequence of this desire to cheer their hearts. Why, he talks, I have often thought, just in the way in which any one of us would have talked to our children when we desire to encourage them! There is nothing about the Savior's language which makes you say to yourself, "What a grand speech! What a rhetorician! What an orator he is!" If any man makes you say that of him, suspect that he is off the lines a little. He is forgetting the true object of a loving mind, and is seeking to be a fine speaker, and to impress people with the idea that he is saying something very wonderful, and saying it very grandly. The Savior quite ignores all idea of beautiful expression in just trying to bring forth his meaning in the plainest possible manner. He sought the shortest way to the hearts of those whom he addressed, and he cared nothing whether flowers grew or did not grow by the roadside. For this reason there is no eloquence like the eloquence of Jesus— there is a style of majestic simplicity about him that is altogether his own, and in this lies unsurpassed sublimity. I now and then see in books quotations, and the names of the authors are put at the foot of the extracts. But whenever I observe that the name of Christ is put below a quotation, I regard it as unnecessary and should be struck out, for there is never any fear of mistaking the language of the Son of God for that of any of the sons of men. He has a style all his own. This, however, is incidental to the design aimed at, for he does not study style of rhetoric in any degree, but simply aims at conveying his thought. For this reason he speaks in simple words, such as those of our text—"The very hairs of your head are all numbered." Your great and learned men will not talk about the hairs of your head. All their discourse is upon the nebulae and the stars, geological periods and organic remains, evolution and the solidarity of the race, and I do not know what else. They will not stoop to common-place things; they must say something great, sublime, dazzling, brilliant, full of fireworks. The Master is as far removed from all this as the heavens are from the most splendid canopy that ever adorned a mortal's throne. He talks in homely language because he is at home; he speaks the language of the heart because he is all heart, and wants to reach the hearts of those to whom he speaks. I commend the text to you for that reason, though for many others besides. "The very hairs of your head are all numbered."

Thinking over these words, they seem to have in them four things at least, and we may take four views of their meaning—and the first is, *foreordination*—"The very hairs of your head have been all numbered." You will find that to be a more accurate version of the text than that which is before us. The verb is not in the present, but in the pluperfect tense.[1] The very hairs of your head have been all numbered before worlds were made. Secondly, I see in the text *knowledge*. This is very clear—God so knows his people that the very hairs of their head are all numbered by him. Thirdly, there is *valuation*—he sets such a high estimate upon his own servants, that it is said of them, "The very hairs of your head are all numbered." You are so precious that the least portion of you is precious; the King keeps a register of every part of you, "The very hairs of your head are all numbered." And, lastly, here is most evidently *preservation*. The Savior has been telling them not to fear those that can kill the body, and are not able to kill the soul. He speaks of God's preserving them. In another place he told his disciples, "But not a hair of your head will perish,"[2] and he intends the same sense in this case; there shall be a perfect preservation of his people. "The very hairs of your head are all numbered."

I. Come then, to the first thought. Here is FOREORDINATION. "The very hairs of your head

---

1 Pluperfect tense—the tense which denotes that an action or event was completed at or before the time of another past action or event.

2 Luke 21:18 (NIV).

are all numbered." Most Christian people believe in the providence of God, but all Christian people are not prepared to follow out the truth which that involves. They appear to believe that there is a providence overruling, but they seem to have forgotten that there always was such a providence, and that providence must be, after all, a matter of divine foresight. God must have foreseen, or he could not have provided, for "providence" is, after all, the Latin for foresight. The provision which God makes is the result of his vision beforehand of such and such a thing as needful to us. Foresight must essentially belong to any true and real providence.

How far does God's foresight extend? It extends, we believe, to the entire person and everything around them. God ordained long ago when we should be born, and where, and who our parents should be, and what is our lot in infancy, and what is our path in youth, and what is our position in adulthood. From the first to the last it has all happened according to the divine purpose, even as it was ordained by the divine will. Not only the person, but all that concerns the person, is foreordained of the Lord—"the very hairs of your head," that is to say, all that which has anything to do with you, which comes into any kind of contact with you, and is in any sense part and parcel of yourself, is under the divine foresight and predestination. Everything is in the divine purpose, and has been ordered by the divine wisdom—all the events of your life—the greater certainly, the smaller with equal certainty. It is impossible to draw a line in providence, and say this is arranged by providence, and that is not. It must take everything in its sweep, all that happens. It determines not only the movement of a star, but the blowing of a grain of dust along the public road. All this is clear from the very nature of the thing. God's providence knows of things so little that nothing is beneath his notice, and of things so great that nothing is beyond his control. Nothing is too little or too great for God to rule and overrule.

All that a person undergoes is also ordained of heaven. The hairs of your head, should they turn white in a single night by grief, will not do so without divine permission. Should you be spared until every hair constitutes a part of the crown of glory of your old age, you shall not be older than God wills. You shall neither die before your time, nor live beyond it. All that concerns you, I say, from first to last, all that is of you, and in you, and around you—

> "All shall come, and last, and end,
>   As shall please your heavenly Friend."[1]
> "The very hairs of your head are all numbered."

And this is what I call your attention to—what

---

1 A quote from *Sovereign Ruler of the Skies* by John Ryland.

is the source of this numbering? It could be that they are all numbered by some recording angel who is set to do the work. It may be so, but that is not the thing we have to consider tonight. This numbering is done by your Father, who is in heaven. The ordinances that rule your life are in his hands, and to him belong the issues of death, and this makes it to be such a happy fact. Fate is hard and cruel, but predestination is fatherly, and wise, and kind. The wheels of providence are always high and terrible. But they are full of eyes, and those eyes look with the clear sight of wisdom, and righteousness, and love, and they look towards the good of them that love God, and are the called according to his purpose. Terrible, indeed, it is to think of things as fixed by an eternal plan, but the terror is taken from it when we feel that we are children of this great Father, and that he wills nothing but what shall, in the end, work to conform us to the image of his Son, and display the glory of his own righteousness, and grace, and truth.

Dear friend, perhaps you are blind! You will feel sweet content in the dark when you can say, "This blindness was determined of my tender and loving Father. I know it was so, since the very hairs of my head are all numbered." Or it may be that you have from childhood been the subject of another physical infirmity, which has caused you great loss and pain, and even now it is threatening to bring you suddenly to the grave. Had this cross been laid upon you by an enemy, you might have complained, but it has been ordained for you by him who cannot be unkind or unjust. Therefore say, "He is the LORD; let him do what is good in his eyes."[1] We are taught to pray, "Your will be done." Dare we contradict our own prayers by kicking against that will? Job glorified God, and yet he spoke no more than he should have done when he said, "The Lord gave, and the Lord has taken away; blessed be the name of the Lord."[2] I always admire in Job his ascribing all his afflictions to the Lord because apparently it was the Sabeans that took away his oxen and asses. It was the Chaldeans that took away his camels. It was the wind from the wilderness, raised by the devil, that took away his children. Job does not care so much for Sabeans, and Chaldeans, and devils, as to mention them, but he cries, looking to the First Cause of all events, "The Lord gave, and the Lord has taken away; blessed be the name of the Lord." When we can get at the back of visible things, and see, not merely the puppets, but the strings that move them, then we come near to wisdom. Wicked beings act according to their own free will, and therefore all of the moral evil of their conduct rests wholly and solely with themselves, but the great God, somehow, mysteriously, quite clear of all complicity with human

1 See 1 Samuel 3:18 (NIV).
2 See Job 1:21.

sin, effects his own purposes, which are always good and right. It is he, who from evil, either real or seeming, still produces good, and better still, in infinite progression. When I say, we get to this First Force, and real source of power, then we get where we learn wisdom, and we are helped in the struggle of life. When we see that all things are arranged by him who orders all things according to the counsel of his own will, then we bow our heads and worship.

The practical outcome of all this, to every Christian, should be just this, "If it be so, that all things in my life are ordered of God, even to the hairs of my head, then let me learn submission. Let me bow before the Supreme Will which should have its way. Though it cost me many tears, and many pains, yet will I never be content until I can say, 'Father, your will be done.'" Human nature prompts us to ask that, if it be possible, the bitter cup may pass away from us, but the divine nature, which God has put into his true children, helps them still to struggle after full submission, until at last they are conquerors over themselves, and God is glorified in the temple of their being. I am sure, my brothers and sisters, our happiness lies very much in our complete submission to the Lord our God.

If you cannot bring your estate[1] to your mind, bring your mind to your estate. The old proverb

---

1 Estate—condition or circumstances of any person or thing, whether high or low.

instructs us cut our coat according to our cloth, and the person that can clothe their mind with the garments which providence assigns them does not need to envy my Lord Mayor in his robes. Joy lies more in the mind than in the place or the possession. The person that has enough, though they have but a few shillings a week, have more than the possessor of millions. The person that is content is the truly rich person; your greedy money-lover is always poor, how can they be otherwise but poor in the worst sense of the word? Oh, it is a great blessing when one thinks that in all the events of providence—God is ordering them all. Then we dissolve our own will into the sweetness of God's will, and our sorrow is at an end!

This I think should, in addition to teaching us submission, always give us such a degree of consolation in the time of trouble that we even rise into something like joy. I was reading today of old Mr. Dodd, who is a person the Puritans are always quoting—a man who did not write books, but he seems to have said things with which other people made their books attractive. This old Mr. Dodd, it is said, had a great trouble, a bodily complaint I will not mention, but it is one of the most painful a man can suffer from, and when he was told that this had come upon him, and that it was incurable, the old man shed a few natural tears at the great and excruciating pain, but at last he said, "This is evidently from God, and God never sent me anything that wasn't for my good, therefore let us kneel down together, and thank God for this." It was well said of the old man, and it was well done that he thanked God most heartily. Oh yes, let us kneel down together, and thank God for our trouble! Is it consumption, a dying child, a farm that does not pay, a business that is gradually leaking away? Let us firmly believe that our God has never sent us anything that wasn't meant to be good; therefore, let us kneel down, and thank God with all our hearts. If your child should come to you, and say, "Father, I thank you for the rod; I know it has been for my good," you would feel it was time to be done correcting them. Evidently the child is not so dull and foolish as to need a sharp awakening by chastisement.[1] They see the evil of their disobedience, and the necessity of chastisement, and now they can be left to follow out the lessons they have learned. When you and I begin to be familiar with affliction, and to thank God for it, we are very nearly getting through it. I believe, myself, that there is a period often set to the sorrows of saints, and that the period is usually coincident with their perfect acquiescence in them. When they are content to have all things as God wills, God will be content to let them have it much as they will. When two wills

---

1 Chastisement—pain inflicted upon a person for punishment or reformation.

run together, our will and God's will, then we shall find a sweet double stream of silver peace flowing throughout the rest of our lives. Therefore, let us come to this—if even the very hairs of our head are all numbered, if everything is really ordained of the Most High concerning his people, let us rejoice in the divine appointment, and take it as it comes, and praise his name, whether our portion be rough or smooth, bitter or sweet. Let us cheerfully say, "If the Lord wills it, and we will it, too. If he has purposed it, even so let it be; since all things work together for good to them that love God, to them that are called according to his purpose."

I shall not plunge into the slough of difficulties which some of you are sure to see lying in the way. I trip over the mire with the nimble feet of faith. I shall not discuss how foreordination can be shown to be consistent with the responsibility of man, and the free-will of man, and all that. I believe in the responsibility of man, and the free-will of man, as much as I believe in predestination. I believe in the responsibility of man as much as you do, and I believe in the free agency of man as much as anybody living. How can I believe both doctrines? I evidently can believe them both, for I do believe them. I have learned this—that the person whose creed is consistent in the judgment of others usually has a very scanty, poverty-stricken creed, and a good deal of it is rather theory than revelation. When you come to make up your theology into a system, you are very apt to act like a builder, who fills in between the great stones mortar of their own mixing. I am content to pile up the unhewn stones, and put in no cement of my own. I will not shape truth, much less add to it. "You will defile it if you use a tool on it."[1] The person who takes truth as they find it in the inspired Book has enough material, and it is all sound. I believe that all the contradictions in Scripture are only apparent ones. I cannot expect to understand the mysteries of God, neither do I wish to do so. If I understood God, he could not be the true God. A doctrine which I cannot fully grasp is a truth which is intended to grasp me. When I cannot climb, I kneel. Where I cannot build an observatory, I set up an altar. A great stone which I cannot lift serves me for a pillar, upon which I pour the oil of gratitude, and adore the Lord my God. How idle it is to dream of our ever running parallel in understanding with the infinite God! "Such knowledge is too wonderful for me, too lofty for me to attain."[2]

Have you ever heard of the inquisitive boy who had been forbidden to go into his father's study. He tried the door, but it was locked; all proper and safe entrance was out of the question. But he could not be content until he had satisfied his curiosity,

1 See Exodus 20:25 (NIV).
2 Psalm 139:6 (NIV).

and therefore he climbed up to the window. To his father's horror, up two stories high, stood his little boy, looking in upon him, and crying with childish pride, "Father, I can see you." What a position of danger for the child! He must be brought down, and taught not to climb there again. Shall we imitate this childish folly? Brothers and sisters, I will not attempt it. I do not want to endanger my soul, and perhaps even my reasoning powers, by straining after the unknowable.

Poor child that I am, I would rather love God and wonder at him, than regard him with cold, intellectual apprehensions, and dream that I know him altogether. I pray to grow in the knowledge of that which the Lord reveals; and I pray for grace to limit my curiosity by the boundaries of his revelation. Surely these are far enough apart for the largest researches. As for the difficulty before us, I do not understand it, and what good would it be to me if I did understand it? I know that whatever a person does that is wrong, they do it of their own free-will, and all the sin in the world I believe to be caused by the willful and blamable choice of the transgressor, but I know that, at the same time, there is a grasp of foresight and predestination so comprehensive that everything accords with the divine foreknowledge and predestination. Let our hair grow as it will, or let us pluck out what hairs we please, let nothing interfere with our absolute liberty in that matter, and yet the hairs of our head are all numbered. So much for foresight.

II. Now, secondly, here is KNOWLEDGE—God's intimate knowledge of his people. "The very hairs of your head are all numbered." Observe what a full knowledge God has of each one of his children. If there were nobody else in the world except you, and God had nothing else to do but to think of you, and there were no objects of his attention beyond yourself, and his eternal mind had no object of consideration but you only, then the Lord would not know more about you than he does now. The omniscience of God is concentrated upon every single being, and yet it is not divided by the multiplicity of its objects. It is not less for any single one because there are so many.

How it should astonish us, that the Lord knows us at this moment so intimately as to count every hair of our heads! The knowledge which the Lord has concerning his people is very detailed, and takes in those small matters which people set down as unconsidered trifles. He knows what you and I hardly wish to know. He knows that which we may be content to leave unknown—"The very hairs of your head are all numbered."

He knows us better than our friends know us. Many a person has a kind friend who knows their affairs most accurately, but even such a familiar acquaintance has never counted the hairs of your head. No man's wife has done that, not even the doctor who has by their long attendance upon us, become aware of the condition and health of every part of our body. God knows us better than we know ourselves. Nobody knows how many hairs they have upon their own head, but the very hairs of your head are all numbered by One who knows us better than we know ourselves. God knows matters about us that we could not of ourselves discover. There are secrets of the heart which are unknown even to ourselves, but they are not secrets to him. His penetrating knowledge reaches to the most hidden things of life and spirit.

Don't you think that a charmingly tender knowledge is intended when we are told that the Lord counts the very hairs of our heads? Does it not suggest how much he thinks of them? There are some who love us very much, and they are always aiming at our good, but God goes beyond them all in a more than motherly care of us, strikingly detailed in its thoughtfulness. We see that his love passes the love of women, for the very hairs of our head are numbered, and that at every period of our lives. Does it not imply a very sympathetic care? When one has a sick child, and watches over it night and day, every little fact about it is known and noted. The darling looks a little pale today, or he fails a little in his appetite; the symptom is anxiously noted. You know how easily love can degenerate into foolishness in that direction, but without any folly, God is infinitely careful and kind towards us, for he knows when we have lost a hair from our head. We cannot make one hair white or black, but he knows when they turn white with grief or age. He understands all about our fading and our growing grey, the little details concerning our body as well as the sensitive circumstances that try our souls. It seems to me—I do not know how it strikes you—as meaning a very, very, very intimate, tender, and affectionate knowledge of us. The fact that the Lord, in this manner, graciously looks upon us, should fill us with joy.

This careful, tender knowledge on God's part is constant. He knows the number of the hairs of our head today, tomorrow, and all the days. He without ceasing watches all the processes which even in the least manner affect our lives. So intimate is his knowledge of us, that our lying down and our rising up, our thoughts and our ways, are all continually before him. And what are we to learn from this? Does it not make life a solemn business? Who will dare to trifle with the Lord God so near?

Do you keep bees? Have you ever taken out one of the frames from their hive, and held it up to observe what they are doing on both sides of the comb? Or have you looked at them through one of those interesting hives, furnished with a glass, through which the whole business is visible? The bees scarcely notice that you watch them, certainly they are not eyeservers,[1] for they are so industrious that they could not do more even if all eyes in the universe were fixed on them. What manner of persons should we be when we know that God is observing us, and noting every movement of our being! What care there should be as to our feeling, our thinking, our resolving, our desiring, our doing, and our speaking, when everything is precisely known to God, even to the counting of the very hairs of our head! What perfect consecration we should maintain! If God so values me, so knows me, that he counts the very hairs of my head, shouldn't I give to God my whole self even to the smallest detail? Shouldn't I give him, not merely my head, but my hair, as that penitent woman did, who unbound her tresses that she might make a towel of them, by which to wipe the feet that she had washed with her tears? Shouldn't we consecrate to God the very least things as well as the greater things? Isn't it written, "So whether you eat or drink or whatever you do, do it all for the glory of God."[2] "You are not your own, you are bought with a price,"[3] and when the inventory was taken, the Lord did not leave a hair of your head out of the record. Certainly he has not

---

1 Eyeserver—a person whose service is performed only under inspection, or the eye of an employer.

2 See 1 Corinthians 10:31 (NIV).

3 See 1 Corinthians 6:19, 20.

left your hair to any of you Christian women with which to indulge your vanity and pride; every tress of it is your Lord's. He does not leave to you men even a part of your talent, of your mind, or of your body; your whole self is altogether his, and he takes stock of it, and expects you to include it in your practical consecration. He observes what you do with little things. He notes even those minor matters which seem too inconsiderable to come under rule at all. We are under law to Christ, and that law covers the whole person.

Shouldn't our belief in this knowledge of us by the Lord, help us in prayer? Don't some Christians pray as if they were informing God about themselves? I think I have heard remarks in prayer which seemed to imply that God was not acquainted with the Shorter Catechism. Friends have even gone over the doctrines of grace as if the Lord was not aware of them. I have heard others pray as if God did not know the experience of Christians—as if they have had to explain to him some of their doubts and fears. When we pray we do not need to explain anything, for the Lord knows all about us, even to the hairs of our head. Dear friends, we have no need to explain our difficulties and perplexities to our God. "Your heavenly Father knows"—let this be your comfort. He knows what things we have need of before we ask him. This is a great help in prayer. It may shorten your prayer a good deal if you go to God with the expression of your desire, and plead his promise, and submit your spirit to his divine discretion. Such a shortening of its length will be an addition to the strength of prayer. You need not be afraid, as if God did not know, but come sweetly to him who knows all about you, and will not act upon your faulty information, but upon his own certain knowledge.

This persuasion will help us to feel that the Lord will deliver us out of all difficulties, for he knows the way out of every labyrinth. He perceives the answer of every enigma. If he counts the very hairs of your head, depend upon it he has a high discretion for greater things. He is a matchless Pilot who will gently steer your way through waves, and rocks, and quicksands, and bring you to the desired haven.

There is so much of comfort in this doctrine of the infinite knowledge of God that I wish every poor sinner here would remember that God knows all about them, and consequently can deal with all their sins and fears. If you want mercy, come to the Lord at once. He knows your way. He knows your position. He knows your broken heart. He knows your weary struggles. He knows what you cannot express. He perceives completely the wrong you have done, and knows entirely the right you desire, for "the very hairs of your head are all numbered."

III. Now, thirdly, and very briefly—Doesn't this text express VALUATION? "The very hairs of your head are all numbered." It seems then, that lowly saints are exceedingly precious to their Lord. Every person of Christ's flock on earth was very poor. If they had a boat and a few nets, it was all they were worth. If anybody had seen Christ in his little church on earth, they would have said, "There is not a respectable person among them." That is how we talk at the present time; as if it were respectable to have money; as if respect did not belong to character, but only to possessions. Yet those twelve poor men he picked out, and he thought so much of them that he numbered the hairs of their heads.

Over there is a poor old man in the aisle, and he has a fustian[1] jacket on; never mind his fustian jacket, the very hairs of his head are all numbered. Over there is a poor old woman who just came out of the workhouse, and she loves to hear the gospel. She is such a very poor old woman that nobody likes to invite her into a pew. I speak to the shame of such pride. She is one of Christ's saints, and saintship is a patent of nobility.[2] If you sold a farm you might count the trees, but not the boughs and the leaves, but if you sold a jeweller's shop, you would count all the pins, and all the diamond rings because everything is precious there. Now God regards

---

1 Fustian—a kind of coarse twilled cotton or cotton and linen stuff, including corduroy, velveteen, etc.

2 Patent of nobility—a document granting the privilege of nobility.

everything about his people to be so precious that he even takes stock of the hairs of their heads. How precious in the sight of the Master are his saints! I have been trying to work out a calculation—if the hairs of their heads are worth so much that God registers them, what are their heads worth? Who shall tell me that? If their heads are worth so much that the Lord Jesus Christ died to redeem them, who can tell what their souls are worth, or rather what they are not worth? They are worth more than all the worlds put together.

Ask a mother what her child is worth. "What will you take for your boy, mistress?" My friends, if she sold him at the price she would consider a fair compensation, all of us could not make up the money if we put all that we have into one common fund. The Lord set such a value on his children that he gave his Son Jesus Christ to die sooner than he would lose one of them. Jesus himself chose to die on the cross that none of his little ones should perish. Oh, the value and the preciousness of a child of God! Worlds would not serve for pence to be the basis of the valuation. Let us prize the people of God very highly, feeling as the Psalmist did when he said, "I said to the LORD, 'You are my Lord; apart from you I have no good thing.' As for the saints who are in the land, they are the glorious ones in whom is all my delight."[1] You please Jesus when you

1 Psalm 16:2, 3. (NIV)

do good to one of the least of these his children. He counts it as if you have done it to him. If they are so dear to him, let them be dear to you—as some of those whom Christ has purchased with his blood are still lost—

> "O come, let us go and find them!
> In the paths of death they roam."[1]

If the hairs of their head are counted, what must their souls be worth? Let us feel that all we can do to save a soul from death is but cheap work compared with the priceless gem we seek. Oh come, you divers, plunge into the sea—the pearls you bring up shall well repay your very great risk and toil! Come, you hunters after souls, there is no such chase as this! Hunt after souls as the brave Swiss man chases the chamois[2] upon the mountains, and let no difficulties discourage you, for "he that wins souls is wise."[3] There is no more profitable purchase than this, though you should lay down your lives to bring people to Christ. How much does God value the souls of his people!

IV. Lastly, here is PRESERVATION. See how

---

1 A quote from *The Straying Sheep* by Robert Wadsworth Lowry.

2 Chamois—a small species of antelope, living on the loftiest mountain ridges.

3 See Proverbs 11:30.

carefully God intends to preserve his own people, since he begins by counting the hairs of their
heads. I say it, for there is Scripture at the back of
my assertion, that none of the people of God shall
suffer in the long run the smallest loss. "But not a
hair of your head will perish."[1] said Christ to his
believing people. If I were to lose a hair from my
head, I should not know it—should you? But God
would know if his servants lost a hair of their heads,
and he makes the promise to them of such complete protection that not a hair of their head shall
perish. Remember that other text, "The Lord keeps
all his bones: not one of them is broken."[2] Now, a
Christian may break the bones of their body, but
in a real and spiritual sense they are free from such
danger, God will keep them—yes, keep them for
all eternity! "Not a hoof is to be left behind,"[3] said
Moses to Pharaoh, and there shall not be a bone, or
a piece of a bone of the ransomed left in the domin-
ion of death and the grave.

When the trumpet sounds, life will commence
for all of redeemed mankind. When Peter came
out of prison, the angel struck him, and his chains
fell off, and he came out of prison, but he did not
depart until he had put on his sandals. He did not
leave even a pair of old shoes for Herod and his

1 Luke 21:18 (NIV).
2 See Psalm 34:20.
3 See Exodus 10:26 (NIV).

jailers. So shall it be with the children of God at last—"from beds of dust and silent clay,"[1] when the angel's trumpet shall ring out, they shall arise, and they shall leave nothing behind. They shall not leave an essential particle in the tomb. They shall rise, body, soul, and spirit completely redeemed of the Lord. "The very hairs of your head are all numbered." Christ knows what he has bought, and he will have it; even to the last atom he will have that which he has purchased. We shall not enter into life lame, or maimed, or having one eye. He will preserve his people in their entirety, and present them "without spot, or wrinkle, or any such thing."

Observe that in the close neighborhood of the text, we read of persecution. Beloved, if persecution should come it cannot really harm you. The three Hebrew children, when they came out of the fire, were not scorched or singed. There wasn't the smell of fire upon their hats, their pants, or their hair. When God's people pass through the fires of persecution, they shall not be losers; they shall go through the fires altogether unharmed—no, they shall win the martyr's palm[2] and crown, which shall make them glorious forever, even if they die in the flames. Therefore, fear nothing. Nothing shall by any means harm you. In the end your sufferings shall be your

---

1 A quote from *We Sing His Love, Who Once Was Slain* by Rowland Hill.

2 Martyr's palm—a symbol of triumph and victory.

enrichment. Though you do not count your lives dear to you, precious shall your blood be in his sight.

Besides persecution, there may come to you accident or sudden calamity. Never be afraid. It is half the battle in an accident, to exhibit presence of mind, therefore let the child of God be calm and composed, for although you should suffer in body, your true self will be safe. Though in the tornado, or in the shipwreck, or in cholera, or in fire, you should be placed in outward peril even as others are, yet your real life is insured by the covenant of grace from all injury. Therefore, rest in the Lord, for you shall be safe though a thousand should fall at your side, and ten thousand at your right hand. If you lose, your loss shall be transmuted into a real gain. Sickness, if sickness comes, shall work your health. God's children have often been ripened by sickness. They are like the sycamore fig, which never gets sweet until it is bruised. Amos was a bruiser of sycamore figs, and affliction is God's Amos to bruise us into sweetness. Maturity comes by affliction. Oh! you say, "I have lost a dear friend." Trust in God, and by divine friendship the void in your heart shall be more than filled. Have you lost a child? The Lord will be better to you than ten sons. Should your father and your mother be taken from you, you shall find them both in Christ, and be no orphan. Therefore the promise stands: "No good thing does he withhold from those whose walk is blameless."[1] "Never will I leave you; never will I forsake you."[2] Trust the Lord when in danger. Trust in him in deep waters as well as on the shore. When the waves are raging, trust your God as well as when the sea is as glass. When the seas roars, and the mountains shake from the swelling of them, trust in Jehovah without the shade of a doubt, for "the very hairs of your head are all numbered." For what reason should you fear? Your vessel carries Jesus and all his fortune. If you are drowned he cannot swim, he sinks or swims with you, for as he has put it, "Because I live, you also will live."[3] If your Lord lives, you must live. Therefore, comfort one another with these words, and go quietly, patiently, happily, joyfully through the world, under divine preservation, since "the very hairs of your head are all numbered."

As for you who are not in Christ, I feel a great sorrow for you, because you cannot partake in the joy of this preservation. As for the righteous, the stars in their courses fight for them, and the beasts of the field are in league with them. But as for you, earth groans to bear the weight of such a sinner, and the elements are impatient to avenge the quarrel of God's covenant by destroying you. All things work together to bring upon you the justice which

---

1 See Psalm 84:11 (NIV).
2 See Hebrews 13:5 (NIV).
3 See John 14:19 (NIV).

you provoke. Flee! Flee! Flee! You have but one friend left—flee to him! That friend, "the Friend of Sinners," invites you to come to him. Hear him as he cries in the most tender voice, "Come to me, all you who are weary and burdened, and I will give you rest."[1]

Come to Jesus; come at once, for his dear love's sake! Oh, may his Father draw you to him now! Amen.

------

1 Matthew 11:28. (NIV)

NOTES

NOTES

MAN'S QUESTIONS & GOD'S ANSWERS

Am I accountable to God?
Each of us will give an account of himself to God. ROMANS 14:12 (NIV).

Has God seen all my ways?
Everything is uncovered and laid bare before the eyes of him to whom we must give account. HEBREWS 4:13 (NIV).

Does he charge me with sin?
But the Scripture declares that the whole world is a prisoner of sin. GALATIANS 3:22 (NIV).
All have sinned and fall short of the glory of God. ROMANS 3:23 (NIV).

Will he punish sin?
The soul who sins is the one who will die. EZEKIEL 18:4 (NIV).
For the wages of sin is death, but the gift of God is eternal life in Christ Jesus our Lord. ROMANS 6:23 (NIV).

Must I perish?
He is patient with you, not wanting anyone to perish, but everyone to come to repentance. 2 PETER 3:9 (NIV).

How can I escape?
Believe in the Lord Jesus, and you will be saved. ACTS 16:31 (NIV).

Is he able to save me?
Therefore he is able to save completely those who come to God through him. HEBREWS 7:25 (NIV).

Is he willing?
Christ Jesus came into the world to save sinners. 1 TIMOTHY 1:15 (NIV).

Am I saved on believing?
Whoever believes in the Son has eternal life, but whoever rejects the Son will not see life, for God's wrath remains on him. JOHN 3:36 (NIV).

Can I be saved now?
Now is the time of God's favor, now is the day of salvation. 2 CORINTHIANS 6:2 (NIV).

As I am?
Whoever comes to me I will never drive away. JOHN 6:37 (NIV).

Shall I not fall away?
Him who is able to keep you from falling. JUDE 1:24 (NIV).

If saved, how should I live?
Those who live should no longer live for themselves but for him who died for them and was raised again. 2 CORINTHIANS 5:15 (NIV).

What about death and eternity?
I am going there to prepare a place for you. I will come back and take you to be with me that you also may be where I am. JOHN 14:2-3 (NIV).

www.ingramcontent.com/pod-product-compliance
Lightning Source LLC
Chambersburg PA
CBHW020445030426
42337CB00014B/1404